Original title:
Odes Among Orchards

Copyright © 2025 Creative Arts Management OÜ
All rights reserved.

Author: Alexander Thornton
ISBN HARDBACK: 978-1-80567-030-8
ISBN PAPERBACK: 978-1-80567-110-7

Epiphanies in the Fruits of Labor

In the trees, apples giggle,
While pears play ponies, quite a riddle.
Plums wear hats, with crowns so grand,
Bananas slip, as they take a stand.

Workers dance with jolly glee,
Chasing bees and climbing trees.
Fruits in hand, they share a laugh,
As cherries plot a juicy path.

Harvest time, a wild parade,
Nature's jokes, so well displayed.
Lemons grin in sunlight's beam,
Fruity dreams—a funny theme!

In the Orchard's Quietude We Roam

Wandering through the green delight,
Where apples whisper, and pears take flight.
A quirky squirrel steals a bite,
While peaches hide, oh what a sight!

Under leaves, the wind can tease,
Tickling branches with playful ease.
Cherries giggle in the breeze,
While melons roll with perfect ease.

We laugh at trees that look askew,
As fruit concocts a funny view.
In this haven, joy takes root,
With every step, our hearts take suit.

The Elegance of Nature's Whispers

A whisper from the grapevine, so sly,
"Watch your step, or you might cry!"
As strawberries tease, and blueberries wink,
Nature's humor is just a blink.

The breeze tells tales of plump delight,
Surprising giggles in morning light.
Orchards chuckle, a silly spree,
As nature nudges with mischief, wee!

Oh, the elegance of slipping on leaves,
Where fruit nibbles bring forth reprieves.
In laughter's arms, we find our place,
Among the bounty, we share a trace.

Reverie in the Orchard Shadows

Beneath the trees we sit and chat,
Discussing how to train a cat.
The apples laugh at every joke,
While squirrels plan their next big poke.

A bee with style floats by to dance,
It seems to have a secret chance.
We wonder if it shares a tale,
Of pollen plots and buzzing mail.

Echoes of Lush Abundance

In orchards dressed in green array,
A pondering pear with much to say.
He tells of dreams of being pie,
But fears the oven's flames up high.

The cherries giggle, round and red,
Each swaying straight above my head.
They whisper truths of fruit affairs,
And play games on the summer stairs.

Serenade of the Orchard Path

Along the path, I trip and fall,
A giggle from a tree stands tall.
The branches chuckle, leaves take flight,
As critters mock my clumsy height.

With every stumble, laughter swells,
As apples keep their secret spells.
The ground does seem to shift and sway,
I'll surely trip on pie someday!

The Sweetness of Forgotten Trails

In paths where pies are born from dreams,
We chase the sun with gleeful screams.
A rogue plum shouts, "Don't take my shade!"
Yet all I want is lemonade!

The shadows stretch, the breeze entwines,
A dubious peach is plotting crimes.
"A picnic thief!" I gasp aloud,
Yet fruit confesses, "It's allowed!"

Encounters Beneath the Fruit-Filled Canopy

In the shade, a squirrel did dance,
Chasing dreams of an acorn romance.
A bird squeaked loud, with a beak so bright,
Claimed my sandwich, oh, what a sight!

Underneath branches, we shared a laugh,
A bee buzzed by, trying to graph.
Who gets the nectar, who takes a sip?
Nature's antics, a daily quip!

A Lament for Blossoms Past

Petals fell like confetti, so grand,
Now they mock me, a sad little band.
Once they twirled in the springtime air,
Now they're stuck in my socks—how unfair!

Mornings were sweet, now they're a chore,
Each bloom just reminds me of more.
But laughter comes from the fruit flies' flight,
They spin and whirl, oh, what a sight!

The Heartbeat of Orchard Moments

An apple rolled by, with a mind of its own,
It bumped my leg, then swiftly was gone.
I chased it around, what fun we'd shared,
A fruitlike friend who simply has dared.

With laughter rippling through the green leaves,
A dog in the distance, sniffing the sleeves.
"Do you smell the joy?" I jokingly asked,
He woofed in reply, no task was too vast!

Where Dreams Bloom in Silence

Under the branches, whispers of glee,
A raccoon dreams of sweet, sticky brie.
I tiptoed past, careful not to disrupt,
His midnight feast—such a quaint hiccup!

Stars twinkled down like playful eyes,
Watching my troubles as they waved goodbyes.
In a world of fruits and laughter's embrace,
I found my joy in this magical place!

Imagining the Orchard's Embrace

In trees so tall, they whisper secrets,
A squirrel steals a snack, how cheeky it gets!
The grass tickles toes, while bees dance around,
As apples drop down with a funny plop sound.

Chasing butterflies, I trip on a root,
The orchard giggles, oh what a hoot!
Laughter echoes from branches so wide,
Nature's playground, where silliness hides.

Rhapsody in the Rustling Leaves

Leaves flutter by like they're in a race,
I'm dodging the branches, oh what a face!
A crow caws a tune, slightly off-key,
While a goat plays the tuba, it tickles me!

Jelly spots on the ground, is that a trail?
Or is it just fruits who've gone too frail?
Nature's a stage, where the absurd takes flight,
Each rustling clue sends joy into the night.

A Symphony of Sap and Silence

In the quiet hum where sweet sap flows,
A worm takes the stage, strikes a pose!
It wiggles and squirms with such grand flair,
As insects join in, without a care.

The sun drops low, casting shadows long,
An old tree chuckles, joins in the song!
With each little critter, a funky beat,
As fruits bop along, tap dancing on feet.

Tales of the Wisteria Veil

Beneath that drapery of purple delight,
A frog croaks a tale, oh what a fright!
He claims to be king of this floral throne,
But I see the bees taking over his zone.

With petals that float like candy in air,
I tried to catch one — but lost my hair!
The laughter of blossoms fills up the glade,
As each little mishap becomes a parade.

Harmony in the Heart of Trees

In the shade where squirrels play,
A bird drops an apple in dismay.
Crickets dance with glee and tease,
While bees wear hats, oh what a breeze!

Under branches, laughter rings,
A raccoon juggles shiny things.
What's this chatter, oh so sweet?
Did a deer just tap dance on its feet?

With every rustle, tales unfold,
Of secrets whispered, bravely bold.
In leafy crowds, let's not forget,
The funny moments we all beget.

Nectar of the Evening Breeze

As twilight whispers on the vine,
A grasshopper sips on sweetened wine.
Fireflies flicker, a comic show,
Twirling around in a twinkling glow.

The wind plays tricks with every puff,
Squirrels wiggle, but that's not enough!
The peach tree laughs with juicy plans,
While melons form a line of fans.

Lemons chatter, zestful and spry,
While cherries giggle, oh my, oh my!
In the evening's soft embrace,
Nature's bounty puts on a race.

The Gathering of Orchard Spirits

The spirits chuckle among the boughs,
As owls debate the best tree to rouse.
Cider jugs are rolling past,
Hilarity ensues at a tree-branch cast.

With whispers of pranks in the air,
The fox dons berries with stylish flair.
It's a party where roots intertwine,
And the harvest moon adds for a shine.

Grapes are gossiping, sticky and sweet,
While plums break into a catchy beat.
Each branch's giggle fills the night,
With fruity fun, a sheer delight!

The Unfolding of Nature's Palette

In blossoms bright, a painter's dream,
Each shade and hue, a burst of gleam.
Rainbow apples nod and sway,
As oranges throw a colorful ballet.

Shady spots challenge all to play,
While rhymes of berries brighten the day.
Peaches spin tales of fuzzy cheer,
As tomatoes jive in peak summer's sphere.

Colors clash in comedic sight,
As nature's brush strokes day to night.
The laughter of fruits fills every field,
To joy and humor, we're all revealed!

Songs of the Fruiting Trees

In a grove where apples grin,
And pears wear hats of kin,
The cherry giggles, never shy,
While lemons roll and try to fly.

The peaches play a game of tag,
With plums that dance and then just zag,
A fruit parade, all dressed so nice,
Who knew a harvest could be so spice?

Hymn to the Hidden Roots

Beneath the ground, the radishes scheme,
Plotting world domination, or so it seems,
While carrots gossip in a row,
As turnips laugh and practice their show.

Silly roots with whispers loud,
Dream of turning into a veggie crowd,
With every bump and twist, they prance,
Who knew a garden could hold such a chance?

Rhymes of Rustic Repose

In the barn, the cows compose,
Melodies that every crop knows,
While chickens cluck in choir's delight,
As goats do ballet by the moonlight.

A pig with dreams of opera fame,
Struts about, but feels the same,
And tussles with a barnyard hen,
Creating tunes again and again.

The Dance of the Cherry Blossoms

Under trees with blossoms bright,
Petals swirl in joyful flight,
The bees all hum a jolly tune,
While butterflies waltz beneath the moon.

Each flower laughs as breezes tease,
A carnival of colors in the breeze,
With pollen parties everywhere,
Who knew such fun could bloom in air?

The Harvest Moon's Gentle Glow

The moon hangs low, bright like a pie,
While squirrels plot how to steal from nigh.
Pumpkin heads nodding in drunken delight,
As crickets dance to the tune of the night.

A ghost in the patch looks for a scare,
But finds only pumpkins with naught but despair.
They giggle and roll, round as can be,
While the moon reminds them of how to be free.

The cider flows smoothly, tickling the tongue,
While apples watch closely, turned red and young.
An owl hoots softly, "It's all just a jest!"
As the farm's sleepy critters are laid to their rest.

So raise up your glass to that harvest moon,
With laughter and friends, it's over too soon.
In the joy of the season, we find our own grace,
Beneath the bright glow of this sparkly place.

Secrets of the Orchard Floor

Beneath the boughs where the sweet fruits hide,
Hilarious critters take laughter in stride.
A raccoon is rummaging, searching for gold,
While a singing bird tries to be brave and bold.

The grasshoppers bounce with a musical cheer,
Announcing their talent, "Come gather near!"
But under the branches, the mushrooms conspire,
To plot a prank that could spark a wild fire.

A low-hanging apple lands right on the head,
Of a lazy old goat who just came out of bed.
He snorts and he stumbles, "What on Earth gives?,"
As laughter erupts from the things that he lives.

The secrets below are more fun than they seem,
In the orchard's embrace, the world loves to dream.
With stories of folly that no one can bore,
We dive in the mysteries of the orchard floor.

The Poetry of Falling Leaves

The leaves are twirling, a dance in the air,
Like a busker's hat tossed without a care.
They rustle and giggle, a colorful show,
While the wind takes its turn, and we watch them go.

The maple dips low, wears a bright cap,
A tiny fast squirrel joins in with a tap.
With nuts piled high, his dance is a feast,
As his buddies applaud with the quietest squeak.

An acorn drops down, with a thud on the ground,
It echoes with mischief, a slapstick sound.
The oak laughs aloud, "That was quite the plop!"
But nobody's here, so they can't make it stop!

As daylight does fade, the leaves drift and sway,
With every soft whisper, the trees start to play.
They tickle the breeze, in a chorus of fun,
Nature's sweet laughter, a day nearly done.

Whispers of the Cherry Blossom

The pink blooms gather for their annual show,
Winking at passers, with a giggle and glow.
Their laughter fills air, like petals in flight,
Spreading joy through the gardens, a pure delight.

A bee buzzes close, quite the comical jest,
It tumbles through flowers, "I surely know best!"
While butterflies flutter, with grace and high style,
They glimmer and dance, with a glittering smile.

An old tree chuckles, with branches so wide,
"Come join in the fun, don't sit there and hide!"
Each petal that whirls brings a story anew,
Of laughter and whispers, and sweetness imbued.

So gather your friends beneath this fair tree,
Where the whispers of blossom set everybody free.
For life is a party; let's twirl and let's spin,
In the joy of the cherry, let the laughter begin!

Enchantment of the Amber Apples

In the grove, the apples grin,
Whispering secrets, coaxing a spin.
A squirrel tried, oh what a sight,
Climbed too high, gave up the fight.

The branches danced in playful tease,
Caught in laughter by the breeze.
A pie was planned, but oh dear me,
Who rolled it down? The chubby bee!

The amber glow lights up the scene,
Pumpkin hats in shades of green.
Each bite brings giggles, oh what cheer,
As cider flows, with fruit it's clear.

Yet in this fun, let's make a wish,
For dancing apples, a fruity swish.
With friends around, it's pure delight,
In this orchard, joy takes flight.

Serenities in the Shaded Glade

Under the trees, where shadows play,
The critters plot and dash away.
A rabbit hops with splendid grace,
While sneaky foxes share a space.

The picnic mat? It's built for jest,
Ants hold court, they'll never rest.
A sandwich flies, it meets its doom,
While bees create a bustling room.

Lazy cows wear funny hats,
As they ponder if they're all chaps.
A belly laugh, a gentle snort,
In the glade, there's joy in sport.

With lemonade, we raise a toast,
To sunny days we love the most.
Each shade a whisper of the fun,
In this glade, we all have won.

Refrains of the Golden Harvest

Oh, the cornfield sways with might,
Sunflowers shine in morning light.
Scarecrows dance, the crows conspire,
Who knew hay bales could inspire?

The pumpkins roll down the steep hill,
Witness the gourd's unexpected thrill.
A harvest fest with joyful sound,
As laughter echoes all around.

Jars of jam, a sticky bliss,
Each flavor's sure to be amiss.
A pie may burst, yet we don't fret,
For messy treats, you won't regret.

So raise a jar of jam so bright,
And toast to days filled with delight.
The harvest spreads its joyful cheer,
With nameless tunes we hold so dear.

Tapestry of Twisting Vines

In twisted vines, we find some fun,
Grapes giggle in the golden sun.
A cat meows from high above,
While bees dip low with buzzing love.

The grapes are drunk on sunlight's rays,
Frolicking in their tangled ways.
A vine that curls, now that's a sight,
As chickens cluck with sheer delight.

The wine will flow, a laugh or two,
A toast to life, to me and you.
With fruity puns and silly dreams,
Each vine unfurls, bursting at the seams.

So let's unwind, enjoy the feast,
In this wacky, joyous beast.
With grapes and laughs, we'll twirl and spin,
In this vineyard, let the fun begin!

A Journey Through Petaled Arches

Under the branches, we leap and prance,
Bees buzz loudly, in a dance of chance.
Apples above seem to grin with glee,
While squirrels plot schemes to steal our spree.

Lemonade flows from the fountain of fun,
As peaches throw shade while we bask in sun.
Juggling ripe fruits, a slippery game,
Slipping on peels brings us tender shame.

Each bloom a giggle, a fragrant jest,
Nature's laughter puts us to the test.
With blossoms like confetti, a vibrant show,
We dance through gardens where the mischief flows.

With every step, a silly surprise,
As cherries drop jokes right before our eyes.
So let's toast to love under skies so blue,
In this orchard of laughter, just me and you.

Scented Memories of the Grove

In the grove where giggles always bloom,
Ripe fruit whispers secrets, no cause for gloom.
The pear tree laughs, swaying left and right,
While lemonade stands prepare for a fight.

Oh, a plump peach, what a slippery score,
Falling right into someone's open door!
The cherries chuckle, bouncing in delight,
As we play tag from morning till the night.

There's a comical dance with bees in the air,
While grandma insists on her apricot share.
The air smells of nectar, sweet as a tune,
In this magical grove where we'll all swoon.

Let's race to the apples, let's claim our prize,
With pie baking contests, we all strategize.
As the sun sets low, we toast to our fate,
In this fragrant paradise, we simply can't wait.

Gathering Light in the Orchard

Sunlight squeezes through, a golden delight,
While we tumble and roll in a burst of light.
With branches like hoops, we jump through the rays,
In this happy orchard, we'll spend all our days.

Hopping on apples, a bouncy parade,
Finding our joy in the fruit cascade.
Lemonade leaks from ripe citrus hearts,
Splashing on us with its zesty arts.

Giggles erupt like firecrackers bold,
In this precious orchard, stories unfold.
Each fruit a laugh, and we're merry fools,
With vines drawing lines of where fun rules.

Beneath the plum trees, we dream and play,
Making fairy houses from twigs every day.
In the glow of dusk, our laughter takes flight,
As we gather joy like stars in the night.

The Quiet Celebration of Nature

In the backdrop of silence, a giggle rings clear,
Orchards invite us, come near, come here!
Beneath a peach tree, we whisper a hymn,
While the old oak winks, feeling sprightly and slim.

Plump berries share their stories untold,
While squirrels debate if the sunlight is bold.
Chasing shadows, we skip through the leaves,
Creating a ruckus, nature never grieves.

The breeze tells jokes with a playful twist,
As flowers twirl, no moment we'll miss.
Bring on the laughter, the chuckles, the fun,
In this orchard's embrace, we're forever young.

Who knew nature hosted such a fine show?
With fruit like confetti in sun's lovely glow.
So let's celebrate our woodland escapade,
In this quiet festival, memories we've made.

Whispers of Blooming Boughs

In the garden, a pear pranced,
Laughter echoing in the breeze,
As cherries danced with reckless glee,
Peaches giggled up in the trees.

A squirrel wore a nutty crown,
He jested with a bashful bee,
While flowers whispered silly dreams,
Beneath their leafy jubilee.

The apples tried to tell a joke,
But wind gave them a ticklish nudge,
They rolled away in fruit-filled fits,
Leaving the pears to hold a grudge.

Oh, the humor of bright blooms,
As sunshine tickles every fruit,
In this silly orchard scene,
Where laughter plays and none stay mute.

Serenade of the Sunlit Grove

Under the sun, a grape sang loud,
A melody of plump delight,
While lemons joined in, zestily bold,
Their chorus brightened up the night.

A squirrel strummed a wiggly tune,
With branches dancing in the bliss,
While the figs swung in merry time,
And promised all a juicy kiss.

An owl hooted like a grand maestro,
But nobody took him quite serious,
As peaches rolled in fruit-some dance,
Causing quite the ripe delirious.

Oh, the jokes the branches weave,
In the grove where sunshine sways,
Nature's concert, full of cheer,
Brightening up our silly days.

Ballad of Bountiful Harvests

In the field where pumpkins glow,
A scarecrow cracked his best debut,
With cobs of corn that laughed so loud,
As if they knew just what to do.

Potatoes played a game of tag,
Rolling round in muddy cheer,
While carrots tossed their feathery tops,
In uproarious harvest year.

Slackers like the sleepy grapes,
Told stories of their lazy days,
Yet still they cheer with every vine,
In this vivid, fun-filled maze.

Oh, the delight we gather here,
In laughs and roots where life's a blast,
Each harvest brings a silly cheer,
It's the fruit that makes time fly fast.

Verses in the Verdant Canopy

In the treetops, giggles rise,
As leaves tell tales of fruity fun,
Berries blushed in cheeky hues,
Underneath the shining sun.

A mischievous breeze whispered jokes,
To the elders, wise apple trees,
They chuckled loud, their laughter swayed,
As acorns danced among the leaves.

The branches wore their best attire,
Curtains of green in playful twist,
With squirrels fiddling on spoons of nuts,
Creating a fun-filled harvest list.

Oh, the canopy above us sings,
With breezy grins and nature's glee,
In fruity verses, life unfurls,
Where laughter lives, and joy runs free.

Echoes of the Orchard's Lullaby

Under the trees, squirrels plot,
Dreams of acorns, why not?
A rabbit hops with style,
Winks at a worm all the while.

The sun peeks through, a golden glow,
Fruit-fueled antics, stealing the show.
Cherries giggle at passing bees,
Hoping they'll dance in the gentle breeze.

Delights of the Dew-kissed Morn.

Morning dew on a leaf so bright,
Ladybugs practice their flight.
A pickle jar falls, what a clatter!
"Who's making salad?" they laugh and chatter.

Sun shines down on a dance of ants,
Each moving like they've got fancy pants.
A rogue grape rolls, causing a mess,
The orchard giggles, oh what a jest!

Whispers in the Blossom Breeze

Petals gossip as the wind whirls,
"Did you see that? A cat in twirls!"
Bees in bow ties, buzzing with cheer,
"Where's the dance party? It's gotta be here!"

A banana slips, oh what a sight,
Fruit salad laughter feels just right.
The breeze tickles blooms in a row,
Nature's jesters putting on a show.

The Fruitful Melody of Dawn.

At dawn's first light, fruits sing their tune,
"Breakfast is ready! Hey, pass the spoon!"
Pineapple jokes about wearing a crown,
While oranges giggle, all round and brown.

A pear tries to dance, but slips in the mud,
Cackles erupt as they laugh in a flood.
With each little bounce, the fruit finds its groove,
This orchard's alive, in the morning's smooth move.

Secrets in the Orchard's Breath

In the orchard where apples lie,
Gossiping squirrels, oh my!
They whisper tales of the fruit's delight,
While birds join in, taking flight.

A pear once dreamed it could be a star,
Instead, it's just a fruit in a jar.
The peaches giggle, dressed in fuzz,
Claiming they're quite the buzz.

Under shady leaves, secrets creep,
While worms throw parties, no need to peep.
The grasshoppers dance, their legs in a spin,
As the orchard's breath lets the mischief in.

So if you wander where the apples grow,
Listen closely, you'll feel the flow.
Nature's laughter, a constant sound,
In this quirky place, joy is found.

A Tapestry of Blossoms and Dreams

Blossoms burst like laughter bright,
Petals twirl in a springtime flight.
While bees wear tiny hats of gold,
And tell stories that never grow old.

A dreamer once planted a seed of bliss,
Hoping to grow a fruit from a kiss.
But all he got was a cucumber lost,
That swore it was worth every cost.

Under the sun, the daisies tease,
Wishing to tango, aiming to please.
The daisies dress in yellow and white,
As butterflies dip in sheer delight.

In this patch of whimsy, shadows play,
Gardening gloves seem to run away.
Join the dance of the fruit and charm,
In this quirky tapestry, nothing's a harm.

Embraced by Nature's Gentle Hand

The trees wear hats of colorful leaves,
While squirrels play tricks, oh how it deceives!
Each branch holds laughter, swinging with glee,
Whispering secrets to you and me.

A cherry once told me it would take flight,
But got stuck upside down for the night.
The laughter of branches, swaying with cheer,
Turns gray skies to blue, brightening the sphere.

In the roots, old stories intertwine,
Of mischief and dance in the warm sunshine.
Grass tickles toes under nature's command,
As life's gentle chaos will expand.

With nature's embrace, the world feels bright,
Even the worms wear smiles tonight.
Join the laughter, embrace the rhyme,
In this twisting garden, we rendezvous time.

Songs of the Ripened Orchard

In the orchard's heart, a concert unfolds,
As the fruits strut proudly, defying the cold.
Apples sing ballads, all juicy and round,
While the crabapples hum, a sour sound.

Bananas try waltzing, slipping on vines,
While oranges roll in their sunny designs.
Melons attempt a jazzy embrace,
But end up in laughter, lost in the race.

The wind plays the flute, rustling through leaves,
Spinning the stories that only it weaves.
With verses of nature, we share in the cheer,
As the harvest knocks, time to get near.

In the ripe orchard, joy's symphony calls,
As the fruit-picking tune flutters through the walls.
Join the melody, it's a sight to behold,
Where the songs of the orchard are endlessly told.

Echoes of Sweet Nectar

In the trees, the bees do buzz,
Chasing dreams, they cause a fuss.
Peaches giggle, apples tease,
A fruit parade upon the breeze.

Lemons laugh with zesty zest,
Pears play tag, they're at their best.
Cherries throw a cherry fight,
Who knew fruit could bring such light?

The plums are plotting quite a scheme,
A picnic dream, a snack daydream.
Orchards promise fun galore,
With every bite, there's room for more!

As sunlight streams through leafy crowns,
The fruit brigade wears zany frowns.
In this grove where laughter grows,
The wittiest punchlines, no one knows!

A Chorus of Green and Gold

The vines are singing jazzy tunes,
Hopping around like silly loons.
Grapes in jackets, ready to jive,
Unleashing giggles, they're alive!

Pumpkins strut with carrot pals,
Sharing tales of veggie galls.
Funky squash in polka dots,
Join the dance with silly plots!

Avocados spin with silky grace,
Challenging each other in a race.
Lettuce cheers from leafy heights,
As garden critters take their flights!

In this bounty, laughter brews,
Fruits in fancy singing shoes.
Underneath the sunny show,
The garden blooms with joy in tow!

Symphony of Petals Dancing

Petals waltz on gentle air,
Daisies frolic without a care.
Tulips twirl in springtime's glow,
Snapping selfies, don't you know?

Bumblebees with snapback hats,
Take a bow on nearby mats.
Sunflowers do a funky spin,
Bringing smiles from within.

In this field, the colors shout,
Nature's party, there's no doubt.
The lilies giggle, roses sway,
Petal parties makes for a great day!

So come and join, it's all in fun,
With every blossom, life is spun.
A floral laugh, the best in store,
In symphonies of bloom, there's more!

Beneath the Orchard's Embrace

Under branches, flat on backs,
Dropping snacks, avoiding cracks.
A quirky squirrel steals a bite,
His little dance brings pure delight.

Beneath the shade, the ants parade,
With tiny hats, their grand charade.
Watermelons turn and grin,
As fruity friendships start to win!

A picnic blanket, spread with care,
Hold your apples, if you dare!
Lemons juggle, oranges toss,
In this space, we're truly boss!

So take a seat, enjoy the thrill,
With laughter echoing, hearts to fill.
This orchard's charm is quite the place,
Where every moment brings a grace!

Serenade of the Ripened Trees

In the garden, fruit does dance,
Lemons giggle at squirrels' prance.
Apples in their shiny coats,
Whisper secrets like little goats.

Breezes tease the hanging pears,
As cherries play on swings, no cares.
A pumpkin jokes in all its glee,
Telling tales of its great spree.

Bees in bowties buzz with cheer,
While radishes try to appear.
The lettuce laughs at all the fuss,
And all the veggies ride the bus.

In this grove, it's quite the hoot,
Where veggies wear their finest suit.
Nature's comedy takes the stage,
In this fruity, funny page.

Beneath the Canopy of Dreams

Under branches where shadows play,
The strawberries sport hats all day.
Tomatoes roll on grassy floors,
While carrots dance with four-leafed spores.

Mushrooms twirl in polka dots,
Cucumbers flaunt their pickle thoughts.
Broccoli leads a merry band,
Together they make quite a stand.

In this realm where laughter's free,
Radishes hold a jamboree.
Cherries swing on vines so taut,
They chuckle at the tales they've sought.

Here, the daisies join the fun,
While watermelons try to run.
Beneath this bough, we all will scheme,
In nature's land of silly dreams.

Harvesting the Sunlit Hours

Beneath the sun with eyes so bright,
Fruits trade jokes in pure delight.
Bananas slip on skins in style,
While pumpkins wink and beam a smile.

Gathering hours, what a sight,
When peppers start a karaoke night.
The cornfield hums a tune so sweet,
With dancing roots and happy feet.

Grapes gossip about the vine,
And sing their songs of perfect wine.
The squash insists it's all a game,
Claiming victory without the fame.

As sunlit hours drift away,
We laugh and play at end of day.
Winning hearts like fruit on trees,
Harvesting joy, a breeze with ease.

The Sway of Branches and Dreams

Branches wave like they're in a trance,
While nutmeg tries to learn to dance.
Olives wink as they take their shot,
And garlic tells puns that hit the spot.

The apples strutted, oh so proud,
While blueberries formed a gossip crowd.
Each leaf a note in nature's song,
As laughter flows forever long.

Here lemons tell their sour tales,
While radishes' truth never fails.
Swaying branches bat their eyes,
As Cabbage Queen begins to rise.

In this place, it's good to dream,
Where all things flourish, love will beam.
Underneath the tangled schemes,
Life is fun, or so it seems.

Whimsy of Wind and Water

A breezy giggle sways the trees,
As birds compete with buzzing bees.
Rivers dance with a playful pout,
Splashing joy where laughter's out.

A squirrel steals the ripe delight,
With acorns donning hats so bright.
The water chuckles, cool and clear,
As turtles play a game of cheer.

Each stream a prank, each puddle a jest,
The nature's stage, where all are blessed.
In this world of tickles and smiles,
Time slips away in the windiest miles.

So come, join the frolic, don't delay,
In this wacky splash, we'll laugh and play.

Grace in the Grafted Green

A tree with arms that stretch and sway,
Tells tales of blooms in bright array.
With fruits like jests upon its bough,
It whispers secrets—can you hear now?

The pears wear jackets, the apples dance,
In this garden, there's a quirky chance.
Tomatoes giggle while peas roll in,
Their green ensemble, a playful spin.

Bees in tuxedos zoom with flair,
Munching on nectar without a care.
Every leaf a joke—oh, what a scene!
In this grafted space, ambition is keen.

Join the merriment, don't be shy,
Under the quilt of a cobalt sky.

Echoing the Secrets of the Soil

The earth yells secrets, silly and bold,
In whispers of wonders that never get old.
Worms hold court in the compost pile,
With roots that wiggle and twist with style.

Old rocks chuckle, they've seen it all,
From tiny seeds to the grandest fall.
Each clump of dirt, a quirky friend,
Sharing stories that never end.

The garlic plants wear hats of green,
In the depth of soil, laughter's seen.
Fungi in capes hold secret shows,
While carrots play peekaboo with their toes.

Dig in deep and take a chance,
Join the soil's mischievous dance!

Heartbeats of the Orchard Spirit

An orchard giggles in the bright sun,
With every heartbeat, it's all in fun.
Leaves snap fingers, rustling with glee,
As branches sway to a tune—so free.

The apples whisper, ripe and round,
With tales of mischief all around.
Cherries pop like fireworks on high,
In this fruity fiesta, we can't deny.

Crisp breezes play tag with the breeze,
The orchard—where everyone finds ease.
With rhythms of laughter, the day unfolds,
In the heart of the trees, magic beholds.

So come join the joy, let's celebrate,
The spirit of the orchard, oh so great!

Melodies of Sun-Kissed Apples

In the orchard, apples grin,
Wobbling like they're on a whim.
The branches dance to noon's warm tune,
As squirrels plot their nutty boon.

With every bite, a crunch and squirt,
Pies may follow, diners flirt.
The fruit's a jester in the sun,
Whispering laughter, having fun.

Underneath the leafy light,
Bees buzz in a frenzied flight.
But beware, the cider's spry,
May cause giggles, oh my, my!

In this haven, joy's divine,
With apples, one can't help but dine.
So raise a cup to all we've found,
In this playground of joy unbound.

Tapestry of Bronze and Green

Leaves rustle tales of days gone by,
While critters scamper, oh so sly.
A pumpkin sports a jaunty hat,
While raccoons plan their next cool chat.

The colors clash in splendid sight,
As apples tease with hues so bright.
In the daytime's golden gleam,
Squirrels build their wildest dream.

Cider flows like stories told,
While laughter bounces, never old.
The wind plays tricks on limbs so bold,
Making the orchard feel like gold.

In every corner, humor spritz,
As shadows dance and laughter flits.
A tapestry stitched with glee,
In every swig, it's jubilee.

The Orchard at Dusk's Embrace

As twilight whispers, dusk arrives,
In this realm where laughter thrives.
Fireflies hold a grand parade,
Beneath the trees, a playful shade.

The apples wear a velvet glow,
And crickets sing, putting on the show.
With every chime a chuckle flows,
For nature's heart is where humor grows.

A rabbit hops in shoes too big,
A jester's cap on its little wig.
The moon peeks through a leafy frame,
It giggles softly, calling names.

Old trees hold secrets and quirks,
While owls hide, sharing smirks.
In this garden, laughter's free,
As stars twinkle in jubilee.

Beneath the Stars of Autumn Light

Beneath the stars, the fruits delight,
With every nibble, joy takes flight.
Cider dreams swirl in the night,
While critters dance, what a sight!

Pumpkins roll with the moon's sweet grin,
As ghosts cavort, let the fun begin!
The wind sings songs of fruity cheer,
While laughter echoes, loud and clear.

Hay bales stacked like characters bold,
Sharing tales that never get old.
Mice with hats and capes of flair,
Join in revelry without a care.

Under the stars, a bountiful sight,
Where apple pies promise pure delight.
So let us feast beneath the light,
In this whimsical, autumn night.

Reflections Amidst the Blossoms

In the orchard where apples grin,
I ponder where to begin.
A bee buzzes, feels so wise,
While I'm lost in donut pies.

Peaches wobble on the trees,
Pretend they're cats, oh what a tease!
Lemons roll like little boats,
And cherries sing, 'We're the votes!'

Under blossoms, laughter grows,
Ripe tomatoes wear funny clothes.
Every veggie joins the show,
Waiting for the new scarecrow.

With every fruit, a joke appears,
Even worms have giggling cheers.
So here I sit, what a delight,
Among the fruits, my heart takes flight.

The Harvesting of Time

Time's a peach that rolls away,
It hides beneath the hay.
The clock's a squirrel, oh so sly,
Stealing seconds as they fly.

Potatoes wear a shocked expression,
As I search for my next session.
Carrots giggle in the dirt,
While I'm stuck in leafy hurt.

The rake's my dance partner today,
Spinning in a funny way.
Every fruit claims it's divine,
Meanwhile, I've lost my mind!

Harvest wisps of laughter bright,
Time has wings, what a flight!
With every bite, a memory,
Just don't ask for the recipe!

The Twilight Gardens of Solace

In the twilight, bees and crows,
Compose a tune in funny prose.
Tomatoes boast of royal stance,
While pumpkins join in the dance.

Twilight's glow, a kooky broom,
Sweeping leaves that swirl and zoom.
Grapes, like siblings, wrestle tight,
As stars corkscrew into the night.

The moon chuckles, shining down,
While cows wear their best frown.
In this garden, all's a jest,
Every night's a silly fest.

Radishes wear glittery hats,
While celery chats with alley cats.
In twilight's arms, let laughter swell,
For even veggies have a tale to tell.

Musing in the Orchard's Embrace

In this embrace, I find a glee,
Where trees and laughter grow like tea.
Grapefruits waltz in sunshine's gleam,
Tickling oranges, what a dream!

Apples giggle in their red,
While I trip and bump my head.
The pears are snickering, standing tall,
Proclaiming they're the best of all.

Beneath the canopy, I ponder,
Bananas slip, and I just wander.
"Who's the king?" the cherries holler,
As I snort and take a collar.

Retro fruits, in colors bright,
Make this orchard pure delight.
So rock your fruits—don't let them waste,
In this fun fest, time's a tasty paste!

Melodies of Blossoms and Breezes

In the orchard, bees dance and twirl,
While flowers giggle, petals unfurl.
Cherries drop, oh what a sight,
As squirrels bounce in sheer delight.

A peach said, "I'm feeling round,"
While apples chuckled on the ground.
Lemonade wishes float through the air,
Inviting laughter everywhere.

Underneath a sun so bright,
Plums claim they can sing at night.
With vines and tendrils making a fuss,
Each berry boasts, "Come taste us!"

As the breeze hums a crafty tune,
Grapes giggle, plotting their moon.
In this merry patch, thoughts bloom,
Life's a party—no hint of gloom!

Reflections in the Orchard's Heart

A funky pear showed off its flair,
While apples swayed without a care.
Nuts exchanged jokes, cracked up loud,
Underneath the leafy crowd.

Cider bottles join the game,
"Press us!" they shout, "Fame is our claim!"
Berries blush at the ruckus made,
While the wind joins in—the jester's parade.

Midst laughter, shadows tickle the ground,
As sunshine plays, swirling around.
"Oh please!" cries the whimsical vine,
"Let's showcase our quirks—divine!"

A squirrel spies snacks in the throng,
Chasing dreams where they belong.
In this heart that beats so free,
Nature's humor is the key!

Echoes of Ripe Fragrance

Mangoes whisper tales so sweet,
While plums roll like bowling feet.
"Who's ripe?" they giggle, "Not me, not me!"
As watermelon sings, "Come taste my spree!"

Peaches giggle on fuzzy thrones,
Waving to their fruity clones.
Bumbling bees crack inside jokes,
Beneath the shade, nature evokes.

Lemongrass watches with a sigh,
"Rind and shine, oh my, oh my!"
An orange grins from branch so tall,
"Life's a banquet; gather all!"

To laughter's tune, the cherries sway,
In this tasting fest, they play.
Echoes of crumbs drift through the trees,
Bringing joy and fruity tease!

Lullabies of the Leafy Labyrinth

In leafy lanes where laughter hides,
Carrots tell tales and humor rides.
Radishes jest, "We're roots so deep!"
As celery dreams, lost in sleep.

Cucumbers dance, wiggling with glee,
Chasing shadows, wild and free.
Zucchini laughs, "Who could be better?
I'm the squash that likes to fetter!"

In a corner, tomatoes say,
"Life's a salad tossed each day!"
Herbs serenade with scents so divine,
"Join the fun, you're part of the line!"

As night whispers through foliage dear,
These garden folks bring everyone cheer.
Under stars, the laughter soars,
In this labyrinth, joy indoors!

Rustling Leaves in the Afternoon Sun

Beneath the trees, leaves play tricks,
Whispering tales of silly picks.
A squirrel winks, then starts to tease,
Dancing round with such great ease.

The sunbeams fall, a golden mix,
While shadows stretch, in silly licks.
A breeze fetches giggles like chimes,
As I chase laughter, losing time.

The branches sway in gentle sways,
Replaying my most clumsy days.
With each rustle, my worries fade,
In this sunny serenade.

So here I sit, and here I play,
Among the leaves, my cares drift away.
Nature's jesters, with all their charm,
In this green world, I find my calm.

Chasing Shadows Among the Ferns

In patches green, shadows run wild,
Elusive shapes of the sun's own child.
I leap and bound, a playful sprite,
Yet trip on roots and lose the fight.

Ferns giggle soft, their fronds a-shake,
While sunbeams snicker in their wake.
I swipe at shadows with funny grace,
But they just dance, a cheeky chase.

A beetle chuckles, 'You can't catch!'
And I agree with a breathless match.
In this game of hide and seek,
The ferns are masters, so to speak.

So I'll embrace this haphazard run,
Each misstep a laugh, a moment of fun.
Among the greens, I find my way,
Chasing shadows till the end of the day.

The Dance of Fragrant Petals

Petals flutter down like clowns,
In a twirling show, they wear no crowns.
I tumble forth, a clumsy guest,
And fall among the blooms, a jest.

With fragrances that tease my nose,
I giggle bright as each one blows.
Like silly hats, they bounce and sway,
In this floral promenade at play.

A bee zooms past with buzzing cheer,
"Come dance!" it calls, "There's fun right here!"
I twirl and spin, a dizzy sight,
While petals giggle with pure delight.

Through fields of color, laughter spreads,
As blooms conspire with quirky threads.
In the dance of scents, I lose my cares,
Among the petals, joy ensnares.

The Orchard's Hidden Symphony

In orchards deep, where secrets play,
A symphony of quirks holds sway.
The apples bounce in comical glee,
While plums roll by, challenging me.

A chorus of critters joins the tune,
With chirps and chortles, morning to noon.
The wind performs with a playful sigh,
As tree limbs sway, a lullaby.

Lemons joke about their sour fate,
As oranges wink, "We're feeling great!"
The bees hum softly, with little flair,
In this lively orchard, music in the air.

So let us dance in this fruity zone,
Where laughter ripens, and joy is grown.
With every rustle, a note is played,
In the orchard's heart, my worries fade.

A Twilight Walk Among the Trees

Under branches, shadows play,
A squirrel steals my snack today.
With apples blushing red and bright,
I dance and trip, what a sight!

The moon peeks through a leafy veil,
While crickets sing a nightly tale.
I chase a breeze, it tugs my hat,
And off I go—oh cheeky cat!

A breeze so gentle, whispers tease,
I hear the rustle of the leaves.
I laugh and twirl, I'm feeling spry,
But what's that noise? Is it a pie?

With each step, joy fills the air,
While owls hoot without a care.
In twilight's glow, I feel alive,
Till bedtime calls—oh, where's my hive?

Bound by Maple and Peach

In a grove where fruits collide,
I found a maple—what a ride!
With syrup dreams and peachy schemes,
A sticky dance in sugary beams!

A beetle bugs me for a bite,
While cherries swing with pure delight.
I trip on roots, oh what a scene,
Laughter echoes through this green!

Maple leaves, like coins that fall,
I gather them and start a brawl.
With fruit in hand, I make a pie,
But eat it all, oh me, oh my!

Bound to giggles and ripe delight,
In this funny orchard's light.
With every step, joy takes its reign,
'Til I bake again—what a gain!

In Search of Autumn's Mirage

I wander through with eyes half-closed,
Chasing dreams where the cider flowed.
Leaves laugh golden in the sun,
While I trip over everyone!

The pumpkins grin, they know my quest,
For autumn's treats, I'll do my best.
I gather nuts and drop my phone,
Now I'm lost, my paths all blown!

"Hey, is that pie or just a dream?"
I follow scents, it seems a scheme.
With every step, my heart's aflame,
Each twist and turn, a new wild game!

In search of snacks and autumn's cheer,
I laugh aloud, no room for fear.
For in this chase, the fun's the score,
I'm bound to munch, forevermore!

The Melancholy of Ripened Times

Oh, ripened fruit, you call my name,
But here I am, a fruitless game.
A grape slips past, my hopes now sour,
I swore to pluck it in an hour!

Peaches pout with a juicy sigh,
As I fumble, watch me cry.
With every slip, a fruit does tease,
"Catch me, quick!" they dance with ease.

Banana peels, oh what a plight,
And pears look down, oh bring the light!
In this patch of sad delight,
I trip and tumble, what a fright!

While ripeness reigns, I find my laugh,
Beneath the trees, I take my bath.
With juice and giggles, time I'll savor,
For in this mess, I'm still the flavor!

www.ingramcontent.com/pod-product-compliance
Lightning Source LLC
Chambersburg PA
CBHW070748220426
43209CB00083B/161